The Snake in t

Part 3: The Tunnel

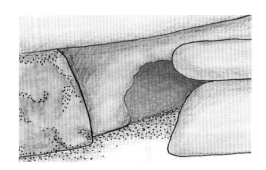

The focus in this book is on the split digraphs

a-e, i-e, o-e *in the words:*

made   snake   cave   races

dazed   cakes   side   outside

like   wide   line   alone   stone

Kevin watches Wellington run across the field. He thinks Wellington must have seen the snake in the cave and he is scared of it.

He goes to the cave to have a quick
look for the snake himself. He cannot
see it. The cave looks empty.

He races back to the farmyard to tell
Lotty what has happened. He finds her
outside the kennel. The two dogs go to
look for Wellington.

3

He is in his kennel. He does not want to
see them. He tells them to go away and
to leave him alone. He needs to think.

Then he lies down thinking about the
snake in the cave with its wide open
mouth and its sharp fangs. Soon he is
asleep and he is dreaming.

5

He dreams that he is back in the cave.

He is looking up at the roof. He sees a

ledge. The snake is asleep on the ledge.

He jumps back. He bangs his head on a
rock. BUMP! He is dazed and dizzy but
he sees a tunnel in the side of the cave.

'Where am I?' he thinks as he goes

down the tunnel. It gets wider and wider

and it soon opens out into a larger cave.

This cave has a line of rocks along one side. The rocks look like wedding cakes made out of stone with water dripping down them.

Wellington goes past the line of rocks.

At the end he sees a large flat rock. A

creature is on the rock. The creature is

a dragon!

Vowel graphemes

ai/ay/a-e: away snake cave races dazed made
              cakes

ee/ea/ie: see seen needs asleep leave dreaming
              dream creature field

ie/y/i/i-e: lies find outside side wide line like

oa/o-e/o: alone opens stone

oo: soon roof

oo: look looking

ow/ou: down out about mouth outside

or: for

er: wider water larger

ar: part farmyard larger sharp large

are: scared